THE BREAKFAST ROOM

Stewart Conn was born in Glasgow in 1936 and grew up in Ayrshire, the setting for much of his early poetry. Since 1977 he has lived in Edinburgh, where until 1992 he was based as BBC Scotland's head of radio drama. He was Edinburgh's first Makar or Poet Laureate in 2002-05.

His publications include *Stolen Light: Selected Poems* (1999), *Ghosts at Cockcrow* (2005), and *The Breakfast Room* (2010) from Bloodaxe Books, and his memoir *Distances* (2001) from Scottish Cultural Press. Most recently he edited *100 Favourite Scottish Poems* (SPL/Luath Press, 2006), a *TLS* Christmas choice, and *100 Favourite Scottish Love Poems* (Luath Press, 2008).

He has won three Scottish Arts Council book awards, travel awards from the Society of Authors and the English-Speaking Union, and the Institute of Contemporary Scotland's first Iain Crichton Smith award for services to literature. *An Ear to the Ground* was a Poetry Book Society Choice, and *Stolen Light* was shortlisted for Saltire Scottish book of the year.

STEWART CONN

❖

THE BREAKFAST
ROOM

BLOODAXE BOOKS

Copyright © Stewart Conn 2010

ISBN: 978 1 85224 856 7

First published 2010 by
Bloodaxe Books Ltd,
Highgreen,
Tarset,
Northumberland NE48 1RP.

www.bloodaxebooks.com
For further information about Bloodaxe titles
please visit our website or write to
the above address for a catalogue.

Supported by
ARTS COUNCIL
ENGLAND

Cover design: Neil Astley & Pamela Robertson-Pearce.

Printed in Great Britain by
Bell & Bain Limited, Glasgow, Scotland.

For Judy

ACKNOWLEDGEMENTS

Acknowledgements are due to the editors of the following publications in which some of these poems first appeared: *Agenda, Ambit, Carapace, Chapman, The Dark Horse, The Forward Book of Poetry 2010* (Faber and Faber, 2009), *The Frogmore Papers, The Herald, The Interpreter's House, Markings, The North, Northwords Now, Origins & Identities* (Bath Literature Festival, 2008), *Poezijos Pavasaris* (VAGA, Vilnius, 2006, trans. Marius Barokas), *Le Sabordage de la Flotte* (trans. Serge Baudot) and *Smiths Knoll.*

An earlier version of 'Off Mull' appeared in the exhibition catalogue *Norman Ackroyd: Scottish Etchings 1974-2006* (Bourne Fine Art). 'Carpe Diem' was read on *The Book Café* (BBC Radio Scotland) and included in *Best Scottish Poems 2007* (Scottish Poetry Library/www.spl.org.uk).

Thanks are due to Mariscat Press for those poems which appeared in the pamphlet *The Loving-Cup* (2007).

CONTENTS

Invitation

A mute equivalent of the bellman's cry
Oyez, oyez invites you to step this way.

Enter by the main portal or if you see fit
slip in by a side gate, keeping a lookout

for tripwires or briers that might snag your hair.
Reassure yourself regarding small carnivores.

No route imposed: an itinerary provided
but which path you take, for you to decide.

If you are chary of rain, here's an umbrella –
and I see you've chosen sensible footwear.

Meal and rest breaks permissible, ideally
through necessity, not to keep ennui at bay.

And no silken twine needed, to retrace
your steps: your own master or mistress

you have exit-points aplenty. So turn the page
and best foot forward. I wish you *bon voyage*.

I

The Duck Shooters

We count the minutes to departure, the train crammed
to capacity. Across the platform another, its windows
blank, is tenanted if at all by ghosts. 'All passengers

please move to the train opposite.' The original
seating plan preserved, but in our new element,
soon in skuffed plushness we are heading south

within sight of the coast, conversation muted
until instinctively we lean forward in anticipation
of the silvery half-circle of the Basin, a glistening

haven for wildfowl and birdwatcher, habitat
of grebe and oystercatcher, redshank and plover.
As we slow to a crawl, mute-swans deferentially

upend. Then when least expected there appears
a pair of duck shooters, discordant in their relation
to land and water. Barrels raised, it is as though

they are looking not into the train but through
its windows and out the other side, the refracted
brightness of sea and sky rendering us illusory.

Conundrum

You'd think there would be a neat equation for how
when travelling by train the view from the window
and in the mirror opposite make clear we are hurtling
away from the past, and into our future, at precisely

the same speed. Simple you say, stating the obvious.
But it doesn't explain how images, as they recede,
may enlarge in the memory; tunnels ahead shorten
or lengthen in accordance with changes of mood.

Even more how an intrusive cell or invisible speck
between sets of nerves can have an impact more
catastrophic than a rock fissure in a mountain ravine;
the tremor of an eyelid, cataclysmic as any fault-line.

The Glass House

has at last been refurbished, its cherished
cupola reglazed, rusted finials restored,

the original design retained in scrupulous
detail along with these statues of skimpy

maidens: Boucher would have adored
the frilly fillies – their dazzling whiteness

once at a visiting preacher's behest
concealed under calico sheets. Today's

speeches receive a quivering of applause,
During the buffet the instruments play

so rousingly we fear for the glass; while the fishes,
back in the main pond, their age anyone's guess,

blunder through whorls of weed, impervious
to plopping coins, the advent of a new century.

Just How It Was

Will there come a time when looking back
we'll say to one another, that's just how it was –
'how it was' being exactly how, today, it is;
the sun at precisely that angle over the trees
in whose shadow a blackbird is being tracked
by a cat, while from next-door's garden a ball
goes bouncing into the lane; the ice-cubes
in our drinks, meanwhile, remaining icy? Even
then we realised that on entering what was still
the future the ice would melt, the sun duly set,
rendering your ribboned straw hat redundant.
And these essential questions: whether the ball
bouncing into the road would reach infinity,
or the blackbird end up being caught by the cat.

Takeover

The apple tree in our garden seems unduly gnarled,
while upper branches have been lopped from others.
And who allowed the flowering cherry to be felled?

The bowls and trays replete with water and nuts
have been replaced by what look like traps
for small creatures. Where our neighbours' puppy

used to play, a large mastiff pads. On the balcony
sit scantily clad figures, neither friends nor family:
did we invite them, or have they simply taken over

without our knowing? Meanwhile an unfamiliar
ring-tone goes on and on. While I try to work out
which of us it might be for, and where you are anyway,

a ladybird lands on my trouser-leg, quickly
assesses the situation, and whirrs off. Watching
its mazy flight, I wish it well. I wish it greenfly.

The Camellia House

Clear as though it were yesterday he sees
the tangled entrance to the camellia house,
its dank water-butt, cracked window-panes,
discarded tools rusting; inside, the glory
of the blooms – each waxen flower-head
symmetrical, the colour of blood.
He takes her one each day in season. Her
workmates, oblivious of the walled garden,
the estate where he rents a cottage, thought
he must be really keen. Only she knew
their origin, that no way could he afford them.

Early on St Valentine's day he found
a scene of desolation, beds trampled,
stems crushed and broken, bulldozers
moving in, blocks of flats going up
where the derelict big house had been.
He imagined droves of young lovers
without two pennies to rub together
kneeling to their partners, purloined
flower in hand – rather than concede
that behind the camellia house, might be
a mound of mulched flower-heads rotting.

Dougalston
(i.m. JMSA)

In those long autumn evenings we played carpet bowls
on the huge lawn, growing so engrossed that our game
would extend beyond even the lingering Scottish twilight
thanks to the insertion of a candle in a pound jam-jar
as a substitute for the jack; the contents of a half bottle
taking the edge off the chill; our efforts increasing until
the hurled china bowls would bound off one another
to be lost in surrounding shrubbery; the ultimate delight
when a direct hit, to triumphant whoops, smashed
the jar to smithereens, extinguishing its flickering light.

Mull of Oa

Kilnaughton beach on Islay is known for its singing sands.
A monument nearby commemorates the loss of a troopship
torpedoed off Oa, in 1918.

On checking my rucksack I realise
I've forgotten my binoculars, and curse
my carelessness. But this releases me

to see what I please. Only when I draw
close does a great woodpecker askew
a telegraph-pole (a first for Islay?)

become a junction-box. A standing
stone is archetypal bull, all brow
and shoulder; another an old woman,

back bowed. Seal turns to rock. A pair
of acrobatic sea-eagles metamorphose
into kites held by surfers in the Bay,

a lesson in grace and muscularity.
At dusk numinous presences
reveal themselves: near the ruins

of Kildalton chapel an early
Christian cross, carved intricately,
and a glistening sky, its mauve and silver

a selkie's skin trailed across the horizon.
The uncanniest saved for last: from
the rocks at Kilnaughton, as a steamer

changes course off the Mull of Oa,
I hear not sands singing, but the sighs
of the drowned, perpetuated in still air.

Off Mull

(for Norman Ackroyd)

Knowing he is sailing from Oban at dawn
I picture the harbour, the throb of the engine
as he plies the narrow channel between Mull
and Ardnamurchan, those pale gravestones
glimmering on the slope beyond Kilchoan,
then rounding Iona, confronting the mottled
grey and ultramarine of Abbey and bay,
mixing his watercolours, applying acid
to a plate, weighing one against the other.

Headland and sea transformed into ribbons
and membranes, contours merge and disappear.
Are these mountains mirages or veils of mist?
Drifts of air masquerade as cliff, then water.
Sensitive to light's constituents and the ghosts
of rainbows, his is an elemental world stripped
of its populace to smash of wave on rock; an eye
so penetrating it conjures up not simply place
but with visionary veracity, the spirit of poetry.

Rain, Rain, Rain
(for Tom Pow)

Your card tells how you and your son,
holidaying in the Hebrides, experienced
'rain, rain, rain, then glory' – triggering
in my memory forked lightning, lochans
thrashed by demonic claymores, a carbon
fibre trout-rod jettisoned on the machair;

or caught in a freak mid-summer storm,
hailstones drumming on corrugated tin,
drenched cattle looming like water-kelpies,
our fleeing helter-skelter for the shelter
of the black house where we were staying,
its thatch soggy under flapping tarpaulin.

Swamped by these thoughts my mind,
seeking the balm of sunshine, is lured
to that baking afternoon at Benbecula
airstrip and the tannoy announcement,
'Would embarking passengers please
remain in the departure area meantime'

while a group of men in black suits
and dark glasses crossed the tarmac
as the incoming plane taxied closer,
then in what might have been a scene
from a Fellini film, stood watching
a coffin being lowered from the hold

and placed in a limousine: all under
an incinerating sun. From somewhere
nearby the stifled sobbing of women
renders us intruders on age-old ritual.
Recoiling from the image and its clarity,
I long for submergence in 'rain, rain, rain'.

Homecoming Scotland

There we were sipping Pimms with a group of Americans
here for The Gathering, when in came such a man-mountain
I swear the room darkened. Eyes like beacons, he told us

he and his tattooed mate were from Austin, Texas. Between
them, they've traced their ancestry to Wallace and the Bruce:
a shoo-in for tossing the caber, or as tug-o'-war anchorman.

Later our host said, 'I saw you chatting to our gay couple.
Bob – the one with the kilt like a marquee – we call him
"the Buachaille". Their ambition's to start up a guest-house

somewhere in the Highlands.' I eagerly await the sight
of those massive hands serving the full Scottish breakfast,
or cradling a clutch of speckled eggs, in soft dawn light.

On the Lagoon

La caccia all'anitra in laguna (The Duck Hunters)
by Pietro Longhi (1702-85): Museo Querini Stampalia, Venice

On the trance-like surface of the Lagoon
a bowman in a scarlet gallooned waistcoat,
kneeling on a cushion, takes aim, the boat
steadied by three oarsmen and a steersman.

Far from targeting waterfowl, the container
of clay pellets in lieu of a quiver is to urge
a team of tame cormorants to disgorge
their catch for the master's supper, after

which, his powdered features at odds
with the others' weather-worn faces,
he will return to his palace in La Serenissima,
having lent an aristocratic veneer to what

is generally a messy and malodorous activity.
No gutted glut on the barge-edge to remind us
of the business of killing, the scene's stylish
portrayal strives to please both eye and spirit.

Gondola

We had seen black keels in the nearby
boatyard but this is crocus yellow, its
seating a bare cross-strut – the only one
we've come across, are perhaps likely to.

Soon, adapted to the span and height
of some gondolier, its braided cushions
and gleaming lacquer-work will grace
the Grand Canal. Guided by supple

muscle, long may it stay the course, ride
the *acqua alta*, above all prove watertight:
our wish for ourselves, too, as we steer
into the current, bearing life's freight.

Early Call

There are days when the fear of death
is as ubiquitous as light...

TED KOOSER

Hearing the phone I am loath to answer,
preferring to be closeted from the world's
ills. But when an upstairs neighbour says
there's a woodpecker on our seed-feeder
we speed to the window in time to catch
its black and white stripes and crimson
nape-patch before it flies off: a few more
rings, we'd have missed it. Now all seems
back to normal...unless the small birds'
shrillness signals the sparrowhawk's return.

Japanese Cherry

Moving house, among our first aims
was to dispose of a flowering cherry
in the back garden we wanted to turn
into a play-space for our young sons.

Rather than see it cut down, a neighbour
took it in, since when it has kept pace
with the one outside our window –
so that face pressed close to the glass,

in season I can glimpse its blossom, pale
peach by comparison. At dusk, almost
ethereal, it assumes a luminescence all
its own, emblem of the soul's migration.

Coffee and Croissants

The young couple at their table
on the terrace have eyes only
for one another, desire tangible
as they share the ritual of coffee
and croissants heated to a turn,
flaky on top, the inside doughy,
butter penetrating to perfection.

In due course they saunter off,
her head on his shoulder, arms
and fingers intertwined, a tender
reminder the morning after
of the night before. Sad were
coffee and croissants to become
no more than mundane custom.

The Breakfast Room

Bonnard frequently placed the most important objects on the periphery of a picture.

PIERRE SCHNEIDER

1

That poster has been on my wall for years.
The other night a woman appeared in it,
a nondescript figure, more a housekeeper
than the wife whom the bohemian in him
painted in her bathtub, over and over down
the decades. Holding a cup, the other arm
slack, she merges with the curtains' muted
tones. A balustrade, shady garden beyond.

Waif-like, half her body outwith the frame,
she seems almost spectral, as if dissolving
or part of a transformation scene. I'd gladly
join her: brioches and baguettes to share,
tea in the pot, a chair easily drawn up. But
unlikely, given her forlorn stare. Not once
has there been a prelude to an invitation,
or the least indication she has noticed me.

2

Whether the artist's wife or his châtelaine
why in heaven's name would I invite you in?
You scarcely endear yourself by dismissing me
as some drab. That, or a moody phantom.
While I make no claim to beauty, a little
sensitivity wouldn't come amiss. It can be
hard enough dispelling the notions of those
who ogle my husband's nude studies of me.

As to not noticing you, quite the reverse.
I'm far too aware of your presence, my room
lit at all hours while you pursue your obsession;

loud music putting an end, albeit temporarily,
to my tranquility. But between marginality
and impermanence lies a fine distinction.
Whichever of us you believe to be the fiction,
I'll look out long after you've stopped looking in.

3

You find my Marthe unobtrusive? For a spell
she was so self-effacing, whenever I wanted
to paint her she would hide behind the curtain.
In one portrait not dissimilar to this she virtually
disappears. Here, simultaneously concealed
and revealed, she blends in perfectly. Small
compensation for what she has undergone,
illness held in abeyance by immersion in water:

hence my depictions of her as Venus emerging,
the light casting a spell on her skin as it was
when I first met her. A vision of young love
preserved, my palette imbues her with the blue-
violet of memory. No need to choose between
smelling the scent and plucking the flower –
painting her has been like bottling a rare spirit.
Now, if you'll excuse me, I have her bath to run.

II

Delivery

Customarily I rise early and spend
a couple of hours in my study before
washing and shaving. One morning
last week, the postman catching me
in night attire, I explained I'd been

up for ages, rhyming away. Today,
exercising, I was perspiring freely
when the bell rang: he eyed me
impassively, then went on his way
murmuring, 'Heavy work, this poetry!'

As if by Magic

Joining the Magic Circle in my late teens
I spent hours in front of the mirror
perfecting my sleight-of-hand, prior
to presenting shows at family parties,
all intent on disguising Illusion as Reality.

Resolved eventually to reverse the process
I disposed of my top-hat and silk squares,
the silver ghost-tube with its spring flowers.
My wand, too, disappeared but turned up later,
tips stained like the fingers of a heavy smoker.

Hoping to reveal through the artifice of verse
something of what it is to be human, yet
loath to claim mastery over how and where
a poem may emerge, I fondly imagined
the wand transformed, plucking words from air.

Challenge

The challenge with art, as with life,
  lies in holding it together;

in keeping your flotilla of paper boats
  afloat, the deeper the waters you explore.

Put another way: the purer the note,
  the greater the fear the glass may shatter.

Electric Brae

When he bought his first car, a Ford Anglia,
my father would drive to Dunure and the Heads of Ayr
then back by the Electric Brae where he'd stop
and leave the brakes off, the configuration
of hill and hedgerow giving the impression
that due to some indefinable attraction
we could defy gravity. Those years now
as remote as though they too were an illusion,
so deceptively precipitous the slope we are on,
by what compulsion of the spirit do we cling still
to the lure of one day again freewheeling uphill?

Fisherman

I'd never have thought my father a fisherman
until driving home that night after the boat
a friend and I were in had almost foundered,
luckily near enough the jetty for us to clamber
to safety, the rain streaming down the windscreen
a reminder how close we had been to drowning.

Only then taking in that he'd been a fisher of men,
picturing him in the pulpit I could make sense
of those gesticulations attending the sermons
for which he was known: conscious of the sinners
in his congregation, he kept casting his divining
rod, covering them and patiently reeling them in.

Comeuppance

Bred in the heart of the Burns country where
my father's family farmed, my early verses

tapped Ayrshire's rich rurality. Yet Burns's
Scots belted out of us, my classmates and I

felt we were the bees' knees compared to those
from 'up the valley' – until the wet Saturday

a Rangers supporter, in uncouth glottals,
yelled, 'Get tore in'ae thae coun'ry yokels...'.

During a spell down south with the BBC,
delivery modified to avert the sniggers

of colleagues at my flat vowels and burred r's ,
I often fancied my shoes holding a layer

of those tilled and fertile acres. Finally
moving to Edinburgh ('...yon great city

that queens it o'er our taste – the more's the pity!')
and confident I could resist its overtures,

on a rare jaunt back to Kilmarnock, over
a pint in the Wee Thack I was charged: 'You're

no frae Killie, you're bluidy English'; distress
at so dismissive a severance from my roots

amply countered by the visionary arrival
of my biblical great-uncle, striding eternal

pastures, declaiming – his voice like a bell:
'Man is from and will one day return to the soil'.

Let There Be Light

Our window-cleaner, a Jehovah's Witness,
comes alone, bringing no fellow-devotee,
the proselytiser in him clearly off duty.
Theology is not among the things we discuss.

He enthuses rather over his other love, golf,
at which I like to think he shows prowess,
keeping his drives on the straight and narrow,
steering long parabolas clear of the rough.

Between visits he has the satisfaction
of knowing that regardless of denomination
he has done his bit to make our lives shine,
each pellucid pane letting Heaven's light in.

Playing Cards with Poulenc

'Manic-depressive' would be the old term; up one
minute, down the next – the source of the tussle
in his *Gloria*, as it veers from riotous to reverential.

Or was it inspired as he claimed by a combination
of Gozzoli's frescoes of angels, tongues sticking out,
and the Benedictine monks he watched playing football?

A pointer to his mood-swings: when out for a stroll
he'd turn his hat-brim up or down to inform passers-by
whether he wanted to chat or be left alone. Some saw this

as attention-seeking: what's more important – the way
you look at the world, or the way the world looks at you?
Perhaps part of a wider pattern: as Prokofiev's partner

at the bridge table did his bids betray his frame of mind;
hearts and diamonds for joy, black suits for depression?
When after a separation of twenty years Prokofiev died,

Poulenc began an oboe sonata in memory of the friend
who had once urged him to enter a bridge contest,
the prize dwarfing anything he was likely to earn

from musical composition. A further decade gone
prior to its completion, its première was delayed
until after his own death – the last card Fate dealt him.

Prizes

Two writers agree that the prize doesn't
matter: one has won it, the other hasn't.

*

At my age, surely no one supposes
I give a toss who wins this prize

or that. Tell them, if the phone goes,
I'm outside – dead-heading the roses.

Sleepless Knight

He shifts uneasily. The turret window, slightly
ajar, casts a slat of light across the four-poster

to reveal his wife sleeping by his side, her silk
nightdress puckered at the neck, and so still she

seems scarcely to breathe. With a sigh he places
a chill hand on hers; overhead her family motto,

'*amor vincit omnia*'. As the weather-vane goes
kiu-kiu like a little owl, or vice-versa, she moans

in her sleep, decorously as is expected of the lady
of the manor. Other small sounds, scratch of quill

on parchment, liquid gently poured, scarcely
register as with a gasp he laboriously raises

his crossed legs to allow just enough room
for the insertion of a small lion to rest his feet on.

Awakenings

When he rose and turned the light on
there it was draped over the bedstead,
a chimera complete with lion's head,
goat's body and dragon's tail. Fearing
the worst he wondered how he could
shield himself from its fiery breath,
only for it to fade away, not the rag-end
of a dream so much as bearing witness
that for their own protection, the least
belligerent of creatures can look fiercest.

Meanwhile she lay petrified, staring
at a tiny fluttering on the ceiling,
not a death's head but some minute
nondescript variety she could obliterate
with a smear of her thumb but at whose
presence her gorge rose, as she recalled
her mother taking the little woollen top
from its tissue paper and how as she put
it on and was buttoning it up it began
to move, full of the eggs hatching.

Snake-Charmer

La charmeuse de serpents by Henri Rousseau (1844-1910)

Such the choisya's golden tonsure, that ivy's verdancy,
lilies like lances, your garden makes me feel I'm in
a painting by Douanier Rousseau – but which one?

How about his hooded flute-player, a glistening slat
of lake, sinuous creatures under a moon of bone?
From his youthful visits to the Jardin des Plantes

he remained on the side of the inmates, not the oglers
and bun-throwers: this taught him to stride the Art world
with a capital A, vie with the vacuous chatter of the salon.

His later work displays gourds like lanterns, the spirit naked
in a silky dawn. But enchantment can quickly succumb
to savagery. Take care, lest you end up trapped in *Nègre*

attaqué par un jaguar; or threat emanating where least
expected, the Snake-Charmer's succulent calf and thigh
clench like a boa constrictor round your throat.

The Visit

Awaiting their arrival, we make sure
the small details are just right, the irises
fanned in their vase, a small ribboned
gift beside each plate. The bell goes.

They are on the doorstep, a tribute to youth
and vigour, unspoken affection for each other
delightfully apparent. Exchanging snippets
of news, we go down to eat. As we chat

and ask when they'd like us to cat-sit, I sense
a growing consternation, not at any specific
breach in communication but some severance
I can't yet place. With no calendar to hand

or notion what year it is, I increasingly fear
it may already be in the future: something
that can be resolved only when we return
upstairs and note which of the four of us

appear in the hall mirror; or if that fails
to resolve the matter, discover prior to their
departure whether they or ourselves pass,
diaphanous, through the inner glass door.

Avalanche

There you were in your ball-gown
with me, wearing an obscure tartan,
sipping champagne in formal gardens
with fountains, ice-capped mountains
in the distance, when there was a roar
as if the heavens had fallen in. Before
we knew what had hit us we were
spinning round in a crazy scottische.

The band, amazingly, kept playing.
As the rumbling ended, we realised
everyone was dressed differently:
fashion had changed, making clear
it had lasted longer than we thought.
We looked older and how can I put it,
somehow decrepit, though no one
was so impolite as to point that out.

Nor had we all made it. Some must
have succumbed in the initial crush.
Of those left, difficult to pair names
and faces, though we can recall our
own correctly (I think). And we've
come to realise that minor tremors
occur all the time. Just that we try,
like children, to tiptoe round the cracks.

Our recurring nightmare is how soon,
though we are not prisoners, we may
need to be roped together: the one way
we can be sure of finding each other.
That's why I make a meticulous note
of everything. But though this is written
in the first person, I still have no notion
whether to file it under Fact or Fiction.

Double-Take

*One of the things about old age is that your memory begins
to go a bit, and also, that your memory begins to go a bit.*
CLEMENT FREUD

It is snowing, of that I am certain. Falling between us
as we stand on the platform, making of her features
a strange pointillisme, if that is the correct expression.

She stands surrounded by bags, a leather portmanteau
and what looks like an old-fashioned hatbox, while
the carriage doors are being slammed. In the old days

a porter would have offered assistance, but these times
are gone. The difficulty, though, is that I've no idea
whether I'm here to collect her, or see her on to the train.

Amidst a hissing of steam, she is instantly enveloped
in impenetrable whiteness. A chance to run for it?
But too late. A whistle blows, and the train has gone.

When the smoke clears, I am alone on the platform.
A poster on the wall of the waiting-room opposite
shows a woman standing amidst her luggage, an onyx

cigarette-holder in one languid hand, her opal eyes
fixed on me in a way I do not begin to understand.
In the background, a train is pulling either in or out,

Back home, and finding the table for some reason
set for two, napkins pressed, a bottle of Sancerre
chilling, it is clear I must have been expecting someone.

But all I can think of is to start thumbing yet again
through my old timetables, to track down which train
she could've been on, and whether arriving or leaving.

Accomplice

Having got this far do I seek a bolt-hole,
strive to stay half a yard ahead
or show a clean pair of heels;

before the feathery irises
on my desktop wither,
the rose-hips turn to mush,

tie my chattels in a spotted
kerchief to an ash-wand,
blaze a paper trail? Better

for you to follow, than retrace my steps;
though perhaps on occasion, that too.
But ought I to be peering

over the celandine slopes at you
or vice-versa? Ideally some sprinkling
of clues will show which fork to take,

the route through the thicket,
where to ford the stream; at last
together to breast the rise.

Meanwhile let us
take once more to the road,
a new gleam in our eyes.

III

The Loving-Cup

The coffee-mug I keep for such occasions
as writing this poem flaunts a floral pattern
bounded by bands of umber, a sticker on its base

saying 'souvenir Firenze'. It replaces one from an earthy
Fife pottery whose handle sheered without warning,
other predecessors having variously had their day –

one pressed on us by a waiter in a Burano *trattoria*
in whose voice we'd traced Edinburgh cadences,
now a repository for pencils and quill-feathers;

another from the University of Western Illinois
stamped 'recycle' and 'contents may be hot';
and a ceramic goblet, smashed and restored, fit

for display only: reminders of places visited, decades
dispersed or, gathering dust, marking our passage
through the stages of marriage. Rarest of all

the twin-lugged loving-cup with our initials
intertwined, unbreakable because imagined,
brimful of memories that can never spill.

Early Morning

You know the feeling – when rising early
and about to start work you become aware

of a distraction: not the customary
juddering of an adjoining water system,

shift of masonry behind the panelling,
nursery rhymes through the wall;

more a slightly asthmatic snoring,
but mellifluous and in perfect rhythm.

Has an inner partition been taken down,
some somnambulist moved in?

I throw open the shutters, let light in.
There they are on the garden wall,

the male cooing like a benign steam engine,
the females all a-do. A rap on the pane

and they've gone, clumsily as befits the elderly.
Next morning they're back, amorous as ever.

This time I leave them in peace. Worse things
to have outside your window than so decorous a love-in.

Arcadia

Having down the years grown accustomed
to the brown-and-white plates and sauceboats
on your kitchen shelves, the other day I took in
for the first time their Arcadian scenes. The *pièce*

de résistance, an ashet eighteen inches across,
shows reclining if not Dame Flora then a near
relation, in a coach drawn by prancing hounds;
behind a Doric arch, a girl with a bow and arrow.

Long unnoticed, they are blissfully oblivious
of the aromas and bubbling pans, never mind
the dinner-talk, the concertos from the radio
on the marble table-top below. But look closely,

on tiptoe if need be, you'll see the chariot
she's in has only two wheels, so that she defies
gravity the way only a beautiful woman can –
and as our lives hope to, through love's sway.

Coolly she ignores the leap to the quarry-tiles
below. Less secure I ponder that given
a sudden tremor, our Arcadia could topple
and shatter to shards on the kitchen floor.

Soloist

Seeing above Glen Lyon a forester
sawing in a shaft of sunlight so far

downwind the sound is drowned
by perpetual lark-song, I am drawn

to that sweltering auditorium decades ago
and Rostropovitch playing Dvorak's cello

concerto; folk melody rising, the soloist
silhouetted in a nimbus of gold-dust.

Beaux Arts Trio

(farewell concert, 30 August 2008)

The head of the man in front blots out the violinist
until easing to my right I can see the bow caress
the strings, the pianist's fingers dance across
the keyboard. Now and then I close my eyes

to take in the harmonies. Each time I reopen them
the page-turner leans decorously over, an avatar
offering guidance. After the interval the man's
groomed outline, tilting slightly, induces in me

unexpected benevolence; while his female
companion sways scarcely perceptibly
to the serenity of the *Archduke*, as Beethoven's
jubilation emerges from darkness. The Trio

then run riot in Shostakovich's *Devil's Scherzo*,
wrist movements faster than the eye can follow;
afterwards no mere standing ovation but a storm
of applause, animated hands moving mountains of air.

The Life Ahead

There's no suggestion we don't know who we are
who have, after all, spent our entire married lives
together. But should that day come when either
of us fails to recognise the other, what would I
salvage as a memento of who we once were?

Sunlit slivers of holidays like those in Provence,
lavender and thyme ladling the air, your
legs dandling from a wooden bridge while I tried
to catch swallowtails with a straw hat; allied
to visiting ancient churches and châteaux, tours

of this museum or that; our clinging together
in an icy wind, on the boat back from Torcello;
your elucidating the emotion emanating from
some Renaissance painting; more mundanely,
walking home from the Usher Hall, through

Edinburgh's New Town; threading these, hours
of reading or contemplation, the unregarded
epiphanies of everyday, visits from family
and friends. Our own lives till now charmed
but more and more aware of others on razor-wire,

given the eventuality I should pray above all
that no harm befall you – but to whom, given
there's no God I believe in? Chary of total denial,
I'd cling to the coward's middle way, though
with no more faith than in the mantra *I love you.*

Thorame

A group of men noisily filling the restaurant
of the little *auberge* in which we were staying,
reportedly a favourite getaway for academics,
sparked off our guessing game. The tall stooper
with the droopy moustaches we designated
to the Sciences; the long-haired one in specs,
Humanities in Nice; skinny Nose-in-the-Air,
Classics at the Sorbonne. What baffled us,
never meeting them on our climbs, was where
their charabanc went, what occupied their days.

Until the morning, rucksacked, we smacked
into them, one working a mini-roller, others
distributing tar, as they resurfaced the track
to the cemetery. They returned our *bonjours*,
and that evening beamed when we appeared.
From then on a shared bonhomie, doubtless
part ribaldry at our being a honeymoon couple.
Memorably on our last night, they serenaded us,
corks constantly popping, as the wine flowed.
The real profs will find them a hard act to follow.

Anchorage

After a recent shoulder operation
two things are a chore: first the pain;
second separate beds, and spending
each night alone. It sends my mind
back to beginnings, to first stroking
your hair, the fine line of neck and
cheekbone; and as night wears on,
to pondering those other places
you can caress a woman, hoping
the time will in due course return.
Till in the small hours I find myself
wondering whether crossing your mind
are such things as pleasure a woman.
Or else I picture you at your computer,
curled up with a book on Florentine
sculpture, or doing one of the many
tasks which preoccupy you daily –
any of them, however mundane, far
more interesting than counting sheep,
and for which I love you, as I fall asleep.

Vanilla

I remember as a boy tiptoeing down to the kitchen,
not daring to switch the light on, opening the pantry
cupboard and raiding the round biscuit-tin, its sugary

contents, customarily kept for visitors, so enticingly
perfumed they made the mouth water. As addictive
were the lavish ice-cream wafers I'd save my pocket-

money for, on holidays in Troon; and years later
the packets of *langues-de-chat* we would chew
while on Provençal walks; the recurring aroma

triggering an accumulation of olfactory cravings
consigned to the misty past when my wife, finding
a new face-cream, started coming to bed imbued

with vanilla – the last thing that as a small boy
(or in adulthood, till then) I'd have dreamed
of penetrating the privacy of the marriage bed,

its association with curve of shoulder and chin
supplanting any return to those airy forays,
boyhood's uncomplicated cure for night starvation.

Homecoming

Trying desperately to think what to buy
that will do you justice – not some tawdry
trinket from the market or expensive item
for which I know you won't thank me – I find
my heart speaks for me: why not a dewdrop

at the point of dissolving; this red wine's
bouquet; a note plucked by that guitarist
on the bridge; or from a minaret in the old town,
the moon's reflection? Impossible of course.
Instead, I stuff my suitcase with fresh herbs,

a replica of an antique cup from the Museum
of Macedonia and, knowing your sweet tooth,
a box of Turkish delight. Only to regain my wits
when it's too late. How perfect, an apple picked
in that garden I visited, crisp and succulent,

with symmetrical on its twig, two glossy leaves.
Even that, I discover, would have been redundant,
given the ample boxful friends have handed in.
Nothing for it but resign myself (no great imposition)
to a cosy kitchen filled with sounds of munching.

Sounds of Music

Sitting in our kitchen as I sometimes do,
ruminating, while you have food to prepare
I become conscious of a sporadic humming,
a series of *pom-pom-poms* which I assume
are coming from the CD you're listening to.

Next morning, during the Haydn trio
in the Queen's Hall, there it is again –
this time more an acoustic reflection,
although mercifully the level so low
it might pass as a sympathetic resonance.

But have the musicians caught on? Every
so often they break off, bows poised as if
for confirmation, then resume their *pizzicato*.
Countering my relief there lingers a fear
that were I to mention it, you'd say I do it too.

What if it grew rife among senior concert-goers?
Imagine at this evening's *La Clemenza di Tito*
a communal humming, swelling to *fortissimo*,
drowning orchestra and chorus till Mackerras
turns on the podium, conducts the audience en masse.

Sir Robert de Septvans

Before our marriage and while working in London
my wife, having seen in *Monumental Brasses of Britain*

an illustration of Sir Robert de Septvans, determined
he would be her knightly companion. On an excursion

to Chartham near Canterbury, bearing black heel-ball,
paper and masking tape, she encountered a benignity

beyond expectation: hands held together in prayer,
ring-curls symmetrical, his armorial bearings three

winnowing fans; slender legs decorously crossed,
feet resting on a lion couchant, mane and tail aflame.

The rubbing when completed she had framed and hung
in our first flat, his demeanour unchanging whether

in my small study or the expanse of the front room
with its television screen and sporadic overnighters.

But a tear, scarcely perceptible at first, ate slowly
into his surcoat, severing his sword-arm. Hesitant

to dump him on a skip, we rolled him in a cylinder
marked SIR, unsure what the future may hold for him

or ourselves, for whom he spanned half a lifetime;
and whose *in memoriam* he may unwittingly become.

Supplication

One blessing in being our fallible selves
as against hobnobbing with immortals

is that when I lean over to kiss you, you don't run
a country mile as you might, were I to turn

myself into a bull or swan, like a god
mad to cajole this or that nymph into bed.

Much easier to get on with it, and fewer
ructions, without like Zeus going undercover.

Side benefits, too. Your not being a huntress-
goddess, I can with impunity feast my eyes

on you without sprouting antlers like Actaeon,
run down and torn to pieces by his hounds;

while you need not fear a vengeful Hera
transforming you, as she did Io, into a heifer.

Now having aged together, the one boon
we'd ask is that of Baucis and Philemon:

may our lives, so long as this does not incur
some horror, end at one and the same hour –

not as they wished, to become two trees,
but that each may escape the other's loss.

Carpe Diem

From my study window
        I see you
below in the garden, a hand
        here pruning
or leaning across to snip
        a wayward shoot,

a daub of powder-blue in a
        profusion of green;
then next moment, you are
        no longer there –
only to reappear, this time
        perfectly framed

in dappling sunlight, with
        an armful of ivy
you've trimmed, topped by
        hyacinth blooms,
fragrant survivors of last
        night's frost.

And my heart misses a beat
        at love for you,
knowing a time will come
        when you are
no longer there, nor I here
        to watch you

on a day of such simplicity.
        Meantime let us
make sure we clasp each
        shared moment
in cupped hands, like water
        we dare not spill.